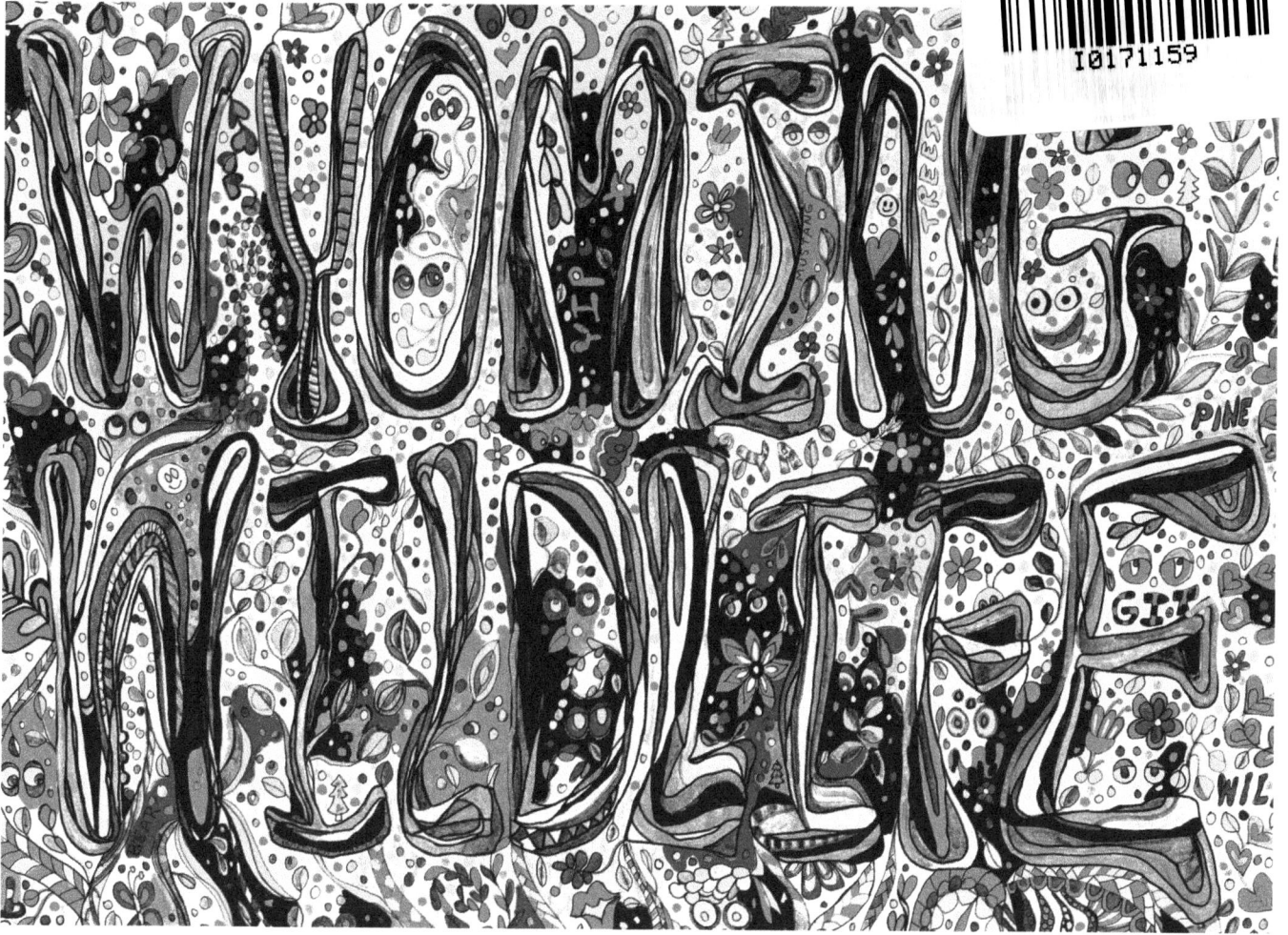

WYOMING WILDLIFE
ADULT COLORING BOOK

Meditate and Relax with some Wyoming Wildlife, including black bear, grizzly bear, fox, rabbits, timber wolf, coyote, rainbow trout, pronghorn antelope, bull moose, deer, raccoon, mountain goat, bighorn sheep, elk, mountain lion, buffalo, and wild mustang.

The artwork in this coloring book is all freehand. There are no computer graphics. I start with a simple pencil sketch, and then hand draw with pen & ink directly onto the canvas., the Old Fashioned way. Unique one-of-a-kind artwork is now yours to turn into your own unique one-of-a-kind artwork.

Kick back, put your feet up, let your mind wander and relax western style. Each artwork is on a single page with a blank back (with a light copyright), and a blank page in between each artwork page. That's for extra protection of your coloring pages. So you don't have to worry about a thing...just take a few colored pencils or markers and have fun!

ISBN: 978-0997455403

COLORED BY:

KRAFT COLOR

◆

Illustrated by Lauri Ann Kraft

WYOMING WILDLIFE
ADULT COLORING BOOK
Western relaxation

Illustrated by Lauri Ann Kraft

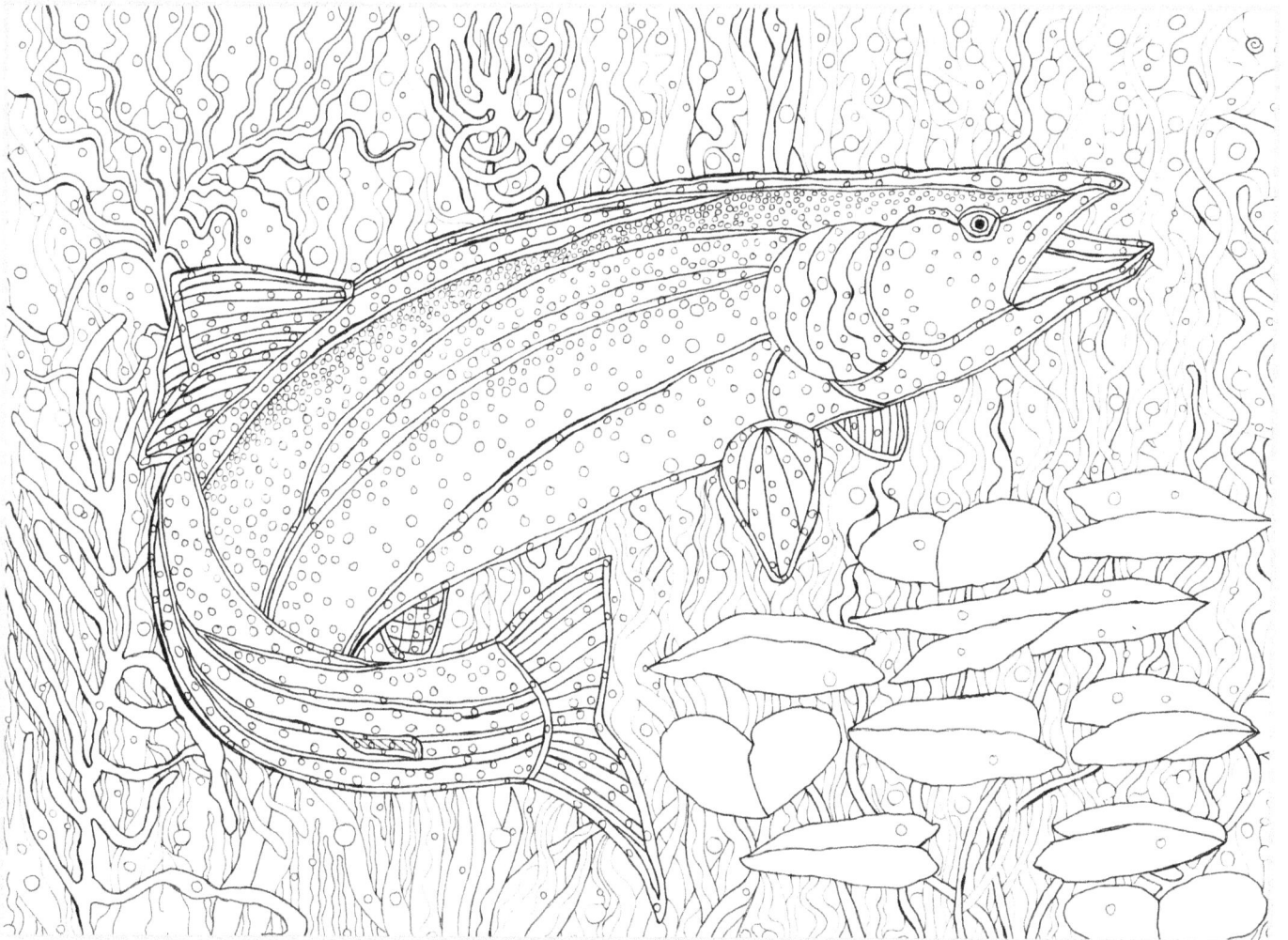

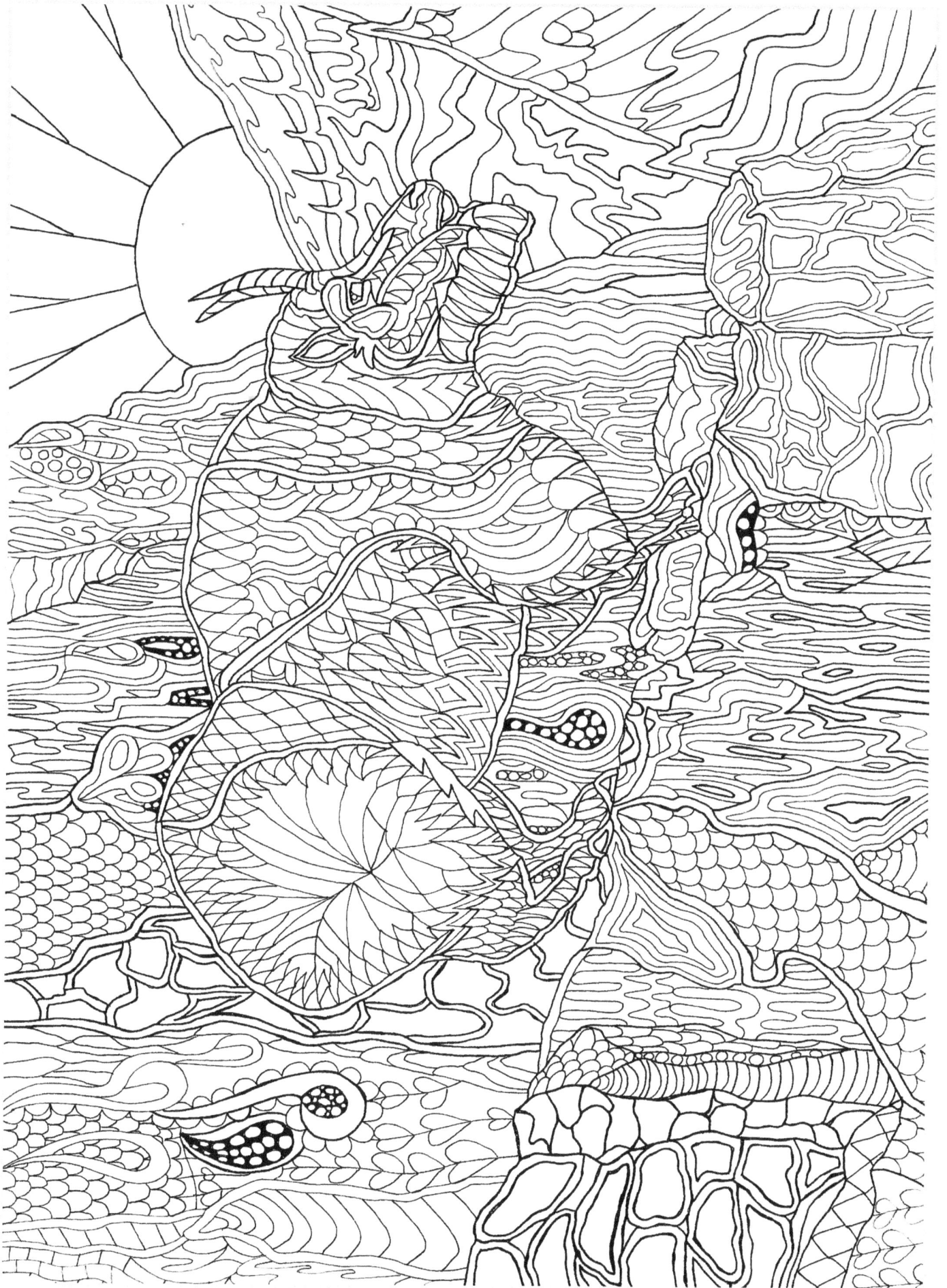

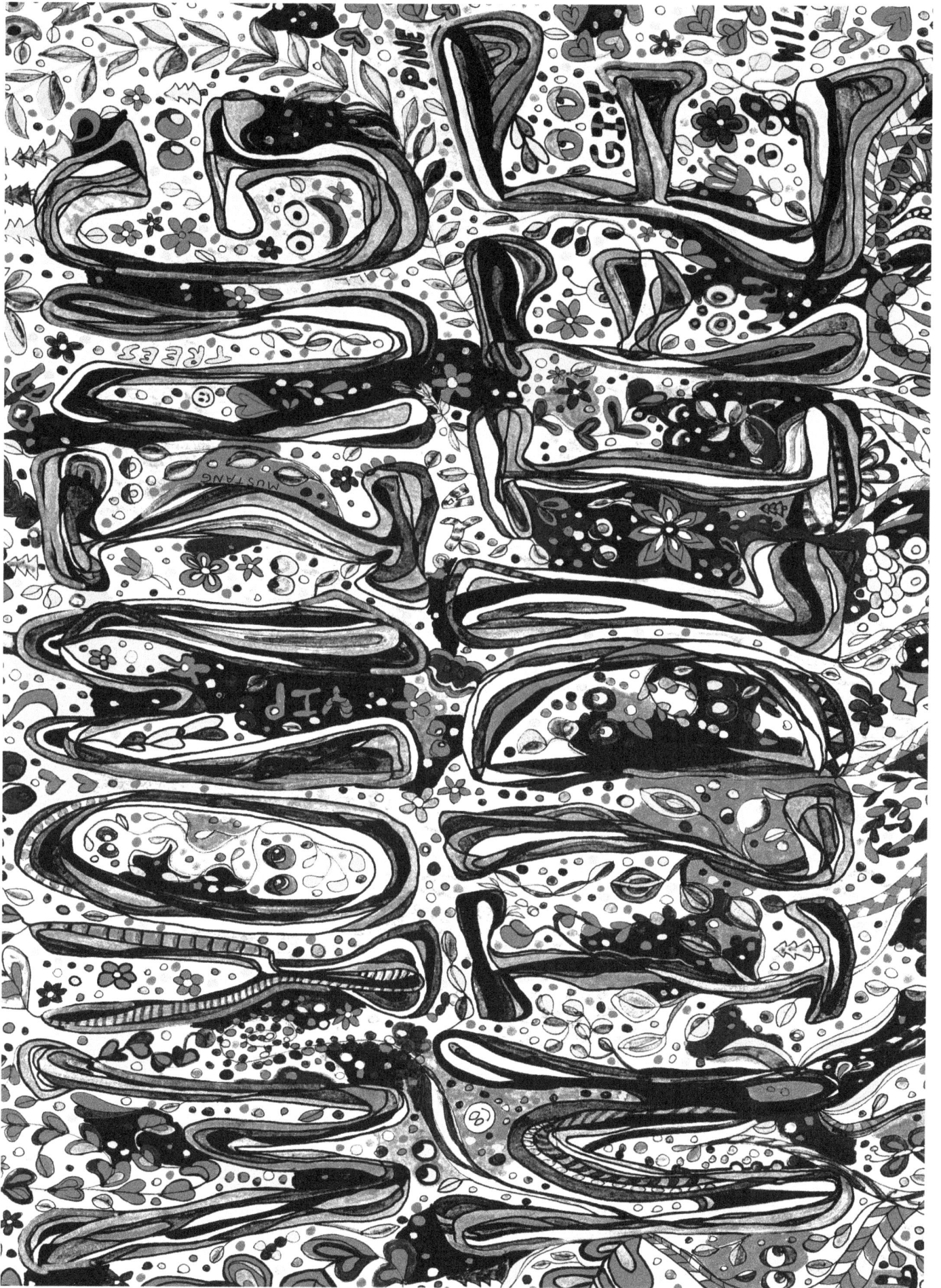

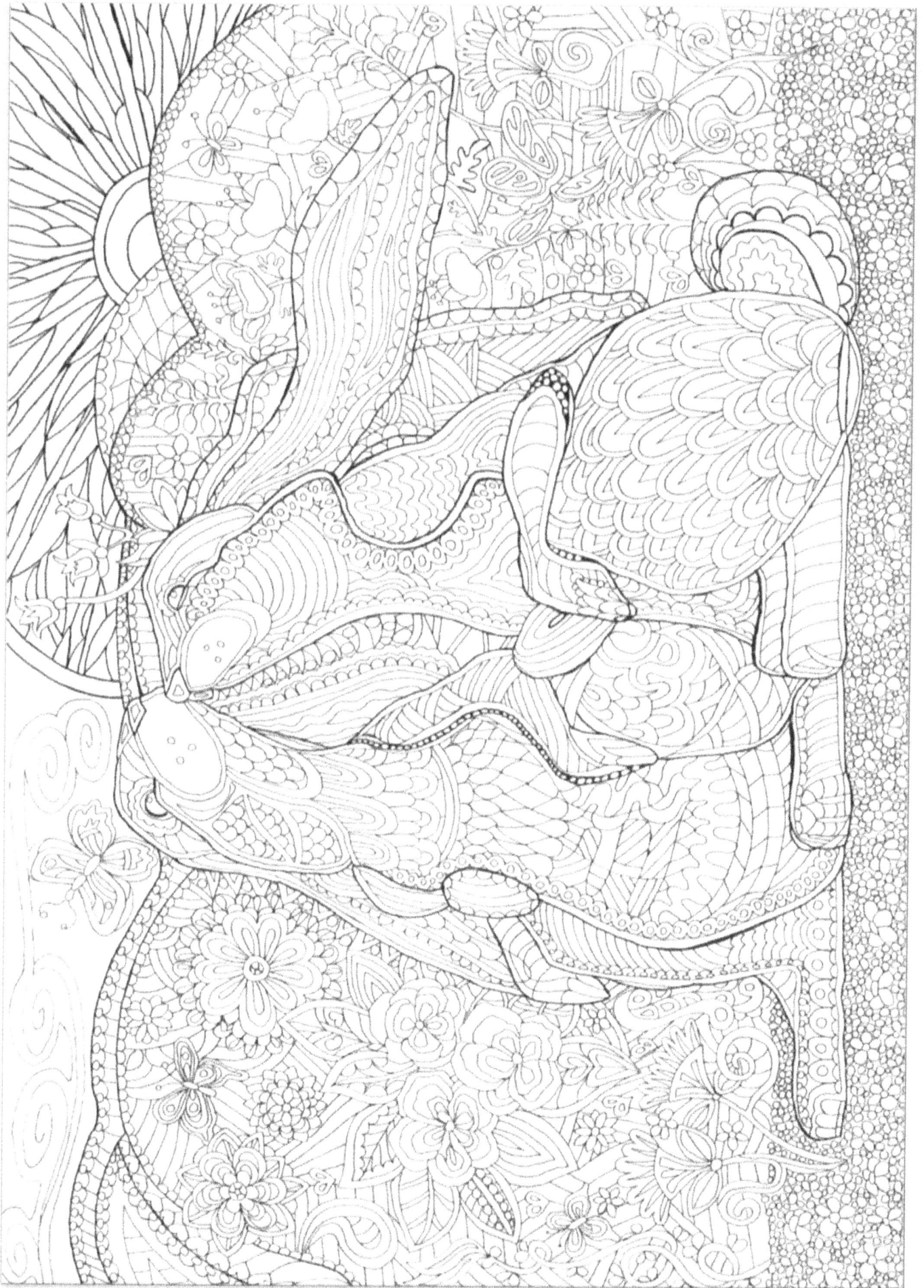

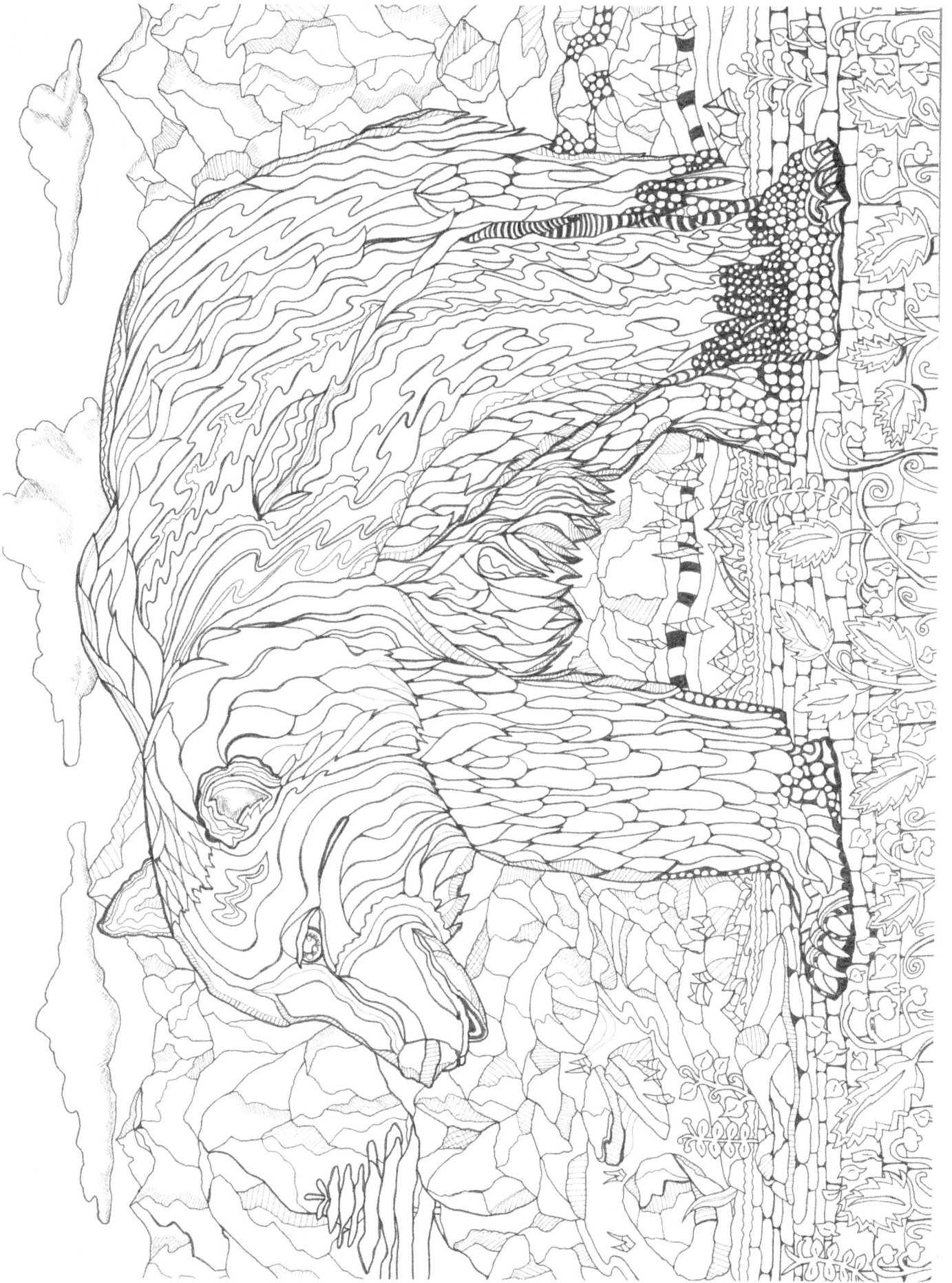

WYOMING

DEVILS TOWER

WYOMING

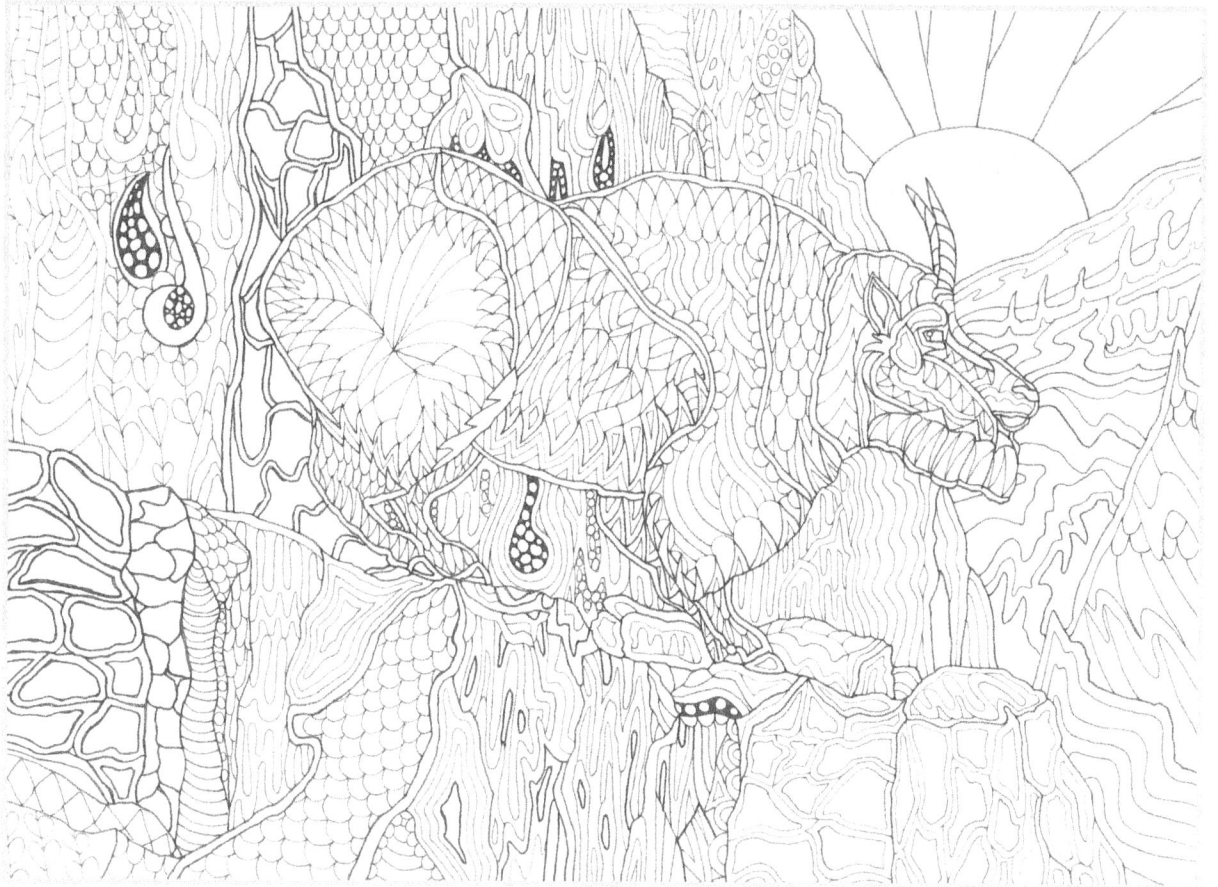

www.ingramcontent.com/pod-product-compliance
Lightning Source LLC
Chambersburg PA
CBHW080551030426
42337CB00024B/4833